BREAK EVERY STRING

Break Every String

Dear David,

*Thank you so much for your kindness.
I hope these poems find you & yours well.*

*Best wishes,
Joshua*

Joshua Michael Stewart

Hedgerow Books
AMHERST, MASSACHUSETTS

Copyright © 2016 Joshua Michael Stewart

All rights reserved including the right of
reproduction in whole or in part in any form.

Photography by Trish Crapo. Cover art by Bret Herholz.

Published by Hedgerow Books of *Levellers Press*
Amherst, Massachusetts

Printed in the United States of America

ISBN: 978-1-937146-92-4

CONTENTS

Born In The USA	1
I	
Grandpa's Knee	7
Squeak	8
What I Knew and Didn't In the Backseat of My Mother's Pinto Heading To My Grandfather's Funeral	9
Another Saturday Night	11
She Called Me Tabitha	12
That Girl In The Newspaper, We Know Her	15
Never Ask What's Under The Bed	16
After Ohio	17
The Wrong Crowd	19
Mother, These Aren't Your Flowers	20
II	
Band Practice	23
December	24
After Ohio	25
Nothing You Can Do	26
Air Guitar	28
Functional	29
Pome	31
Blues 13	32
We Walk The Grounds	36
Father, Sitting At The Kitchen Table In The Dark	37
After Ohio	38
Internal Bleeding	39

III

Love You Like Bread	43
After Ohio	45
Dave Brubeck	46
Stay	47
After Ohio	49
My Grandpa's Banjo	50
Heaven In The Devil's House	52
If You Must Ask	53
Two Teenage Boys At A Picnic Table	55
Strength Training	56

IV

Snow Angels	59
Mother, The Late-December Sun Is An Old Man	60
January	61
After Ohio	62
Torture, Brother	63
Watercolor On Canvas	64
Something To Do With Vulnerability	65
Harsh Winter	66
Reach	67

V

Love Music	71
We Call It Us	72
I Wanted To Be a Blue Jay or Wear a Flowered Apron	73
Devolution	75
'Round Midnight	76
November Morning, He Comes Back Unexpectedly	78
After Ohio	79
My Brother's Son	80
I Tried To Hate You but Love You Just the Same	82
Once Again Lake Erie	84
Ghost Notes	85

BREAK EVERY STRING

BORN IN THE USA

We were pumping our fists with Springsteen,
chanting the chorus as Reagan galloped
the campaign trail, still pretending
to be a cowboy, and the old man who lived

in the blue house with the white fence
lined with rosebushes was handing out mints
from a bowl made out of a buffalo skull.
Uncle Bob chopped off his thumbs

in a metal press on his first day on the job.
My father returned to Khe Sahn sleepwalking
past our bedrooms, shouting out the names
of smoke and moon. *He had a woman he loved*

in Saigon, sang The Boss. Across the bay—
Ferris wheel lights and roller coaster screams.
Child Services found my grandmother unfit
to adopt. An ambulance in front of the blue house

with the white fence lined with rosebushes.
A white sheet. The bones and feathers
of a dead seagull—a ship wreck
on a rocky shore lapped by green waves.

On their lunch break, my father, my uncles,
and both my grandfathers, their names
embroidered on their grease-stained shirts,
stepped out of the factory and coughed up

their paychecks to their wives idling in Regals,
Novas, and Gremlins. *Out by the gas fires
of the refinery.* My father's handlebar mustache
terrified me. My brother built me castles

out of blankets and chairs, larger than the house
that confined them. Taught me how to leap
off the couch like Jimmy "Superfly" Snuka,
how to moonwalk and breakdance. He'd go on

to teach me that disappointment's a carcinogen.
My father took cover behind the Lay-Z-boy
in his underwear. My grandmother offered
a pregnant runaway a place to stay in exchange

for her baby. When the plant relocated to Mexico,
my father brought home a pink slip heavier
than a Huey Hog. The rosebushes became thorny
switches. Over ham steaks and mashed potatoes,

our parents poured out their divorce.
We had to decide who we wanted to live
with before leaving the table. I'd go
wherever my brother went: that meant Mom.

My father took a job out of state.
My mother took a boyfriend, who
dragged his unemployment into a bar
called *The Pit*, then staggered

into our house knocking over houseplants,
and I was the one ordered to clean
the carpets with the wet/dry vac. We'd sneak
out of the house at 3AM to swim

in the neighbor's pool, or ping rocks
off hurtling freight trains. The city condemned
the blue house with the paint-chipped fence.
My mother's eye, blackened. We slept in parks,

better than home. She stood at the sink,
sobbed, scrubbed blood-splotches
out of her white jacket with a soapy sponge.
Wouldn't press charges. My brother bought

a dime bag and a revolver from a guy named Kool-Aid.
My mother was crowned a welfare queen, and drove
a Cadillac assembled out of political mythology.
I smoked my first joint on the roof of a movie theater

with my brother and the stars. An after-school ritual:
stepping over the passed-out boyfriend to grab
a Coke out of the fridge. We spray-painted
gang insignias across the boarded-up windows

of the blue house with splintered teeth. The boyfriend
could whip up one hell of an omelet. We didn't hate
him on Sunday mornings. My mother's stiches.
We swiped a bottle of Mad Dog, drank it while eating

peanut butter & jelly sandwiches. My mother stashed
bottles of gin in the leather boots my father bought
for their last Christmas together. Twice they called
me into the principal's office because a knife fell out

of my pocket at recess. We turned abandoned factories
into playgrounds, busted out the windows with tornadic rage.
Somebody was asking for it, and somebody was going to get it.
I overheard a teacher tell my mother, "He's going to grow up

to kill somebody." Thanks to the Black Panthers,
this white boy had free breakfast at school.
My brother waited until the boyfriend was drunk
on the toilet to burst in swinging a baseball bat.

Later that night while taking a bath, I fished
out a tooth biting me in the ass. Backhoes
and bulldozers devoured the blue house
with the collapsing roof. We rewound

and played back the catastrophic loss
that plumed over Cape Canaveral
on our VCRs. The boyfriend slammed
a stolen van into a tree. She'd pour me

a bowl of Cheerios, pour herself a scotch.
The boyfriend's dentist kept good records.
"I'm sending you to your father."
Son don't you understand now? Front-page news:

firefighters dousing the mangled inferno.
Got in a little hometown jam.
I stood before a judge, pled guilty to
shoplifting Christmas lights, the kind that twinkle.

I

GRANDPA'S KNEE

He knew the boogieman,
nodded toward the barn's broken mouth—
we could visit anytime we wished.

My grandfather taunted us
with the voice of a striking match,
with false teeth, too small for his yawn,

incisors shaped like flames,
that he kept in his sock drawer,
a tongue made of smoke.

We never called him by name
or looked him in the eye
or held our plastic forks like daggers.

My grandfather died with his ribcage
between the ground and a tractor engine,
the fat wheel slowly rotating under a cloud.

I once made a suit of armor out of tinfoil,
stomped off into the woods to slay dragons,
    and I've yet to return.

SQUEAK

From the screen door she shouted. *Just throw it behind the goddamn woodpile.* A frantic moth shimmied for its incandescent god as the boy drove the spade into the damp earth. She shook her head, clicked her tongue. *Do what you want, but leave your filthy boots on the porch.*

Crickets chanted. Trees swayed, Holy Rollers in the wind. The boy dropped to his knees and with angry fingers yanked out a root like a bad tooth before pulling a velvet box from beneath his jacket. He placed the small body inside and latched the lid.

Afterwards, he steadied the door so it wouldn't thwack. Behind the fridge, another trap smeared with peanut butter. The fluff of her hair poked from behind her chair. Someone on TV pitched something indispensable for $19.95. The boy crept upstairs.

In the morning, she slammed skillets on the electric stove. Grease splattered and burned the tops of her hands. She called from the foot of the stairs. *Get your ass out of bed.*

The floorboards didn't thud. No rusty yawn of bedsprings or breaking light from under the bedroom door. She stomped onto the back porch, and squeezed out his name. Birds twittered. In the branches of an oak her favorite necklaces, gleaming like icicles.

WHAT I KNEW, AND DIDN'T, IN THE BACKSEAT OF MY MOTHER'S PINTO HEADING TO MY GRANDFATHER'S FUNERAL

Bugs Bunny coloring book
on the floor. George Jones
on the radio, the first time
I wore a tie. I never saw
a real live dead person before.
Would I see the slits in his neck
where they drained his blood?
Do they really sew their mouths
shut? Would he come back
from the dead to tap
on my bedroom window
if I refused to kiss him
at the wake? If I spilled
my Coke on my good clothes
would my mother turn
the car around?
              I see now nothing
would've prevented her
from looking into that casket,
holding her father's cold hands,
and telling him what a heartless
son-of-a-bitch he was, no forgiving
the years he crawled into her bed,
pressing a finger to his lips,
how he used her love for him
to bait and snare.
               Through Amish
Country, Chillicothe and Aberdeen,

over the bridge into Kentucky,
she didn't respond to my voice,
or meet my eyes in the rearview mirror.
I was a ghost competing with the ghost
riding shotgun, and like a champ
I handled it with all the know-how
an eight-year-old could muster:
I stuck my head out of the car, and let
the cow-pie-wind blow through my hair.

ANOTHER SATURDAY NIGHT

I'm eleven, pacing the living room
in the dark. I'm pressing a washcloth
against the two-inch gash on my elbow.
Mom's across town inhaling barroom

loneliness. Blood and water trickle
down my arm to the studded wristband
my brother, sixteen and god, made for me.
He's joyriding in the Firebird with the mullets

who'll become his pallbearers. I'm yelling
for them until the back of my eyes hurt,
until I stick two Band-Aids on my wound,
and crawl into bed with the scarring.

SHE CALLED ME TABITHA

I

Five-years old, I was giddy
at the wheel of the blue Nova

while Grandma worked
the pedals to K-mart until

she said, *On the way home
from the movies one night,*

*your grandfather threw
me out of a moving car.*

All I wanted was a baby.
She used to cradle me, watching

her soaps. I'd suck her nicotine
fingers until sleep took me.

She wanted a girl, put me
in a dress, ribbons in my hair,

and snapped Polaroids that my brother
dangled over my head for years.

Someone bumped into a stroller,
crashed the baby down the stairs

years before she bought the place.
Now its ghost lives in the basement.

*I've heard it crying. Your uncle was drunk,
watching Rockford Files, but I heard it.*

I wanted to write even before I could read.
I'd tell Grandma stories that she'd jot down

on a yellow legal pad to show my mother
when she came to pick me up after work.

What story you got for me today? Grandma
would ask. *Once there was a dead baby...*

II

Grandma took in a pregnant runaway:
free room and board, medical bills,

but you'll have to give me your baby.
One day Grandma was alone in the kitchen,

leaning over her solitaire cards and the next
the two of them were burning holes

in the vinyl tablecloth with their Winstons.
Everything about Angie, from her frayed

purple robe to the corners of her mouth,
resembled a tired bathmat. Even her eyes

looked like they'd been stepped on.
Mostly, I remember holding my ears

a lot, and hating the baby
because I couldn't hear my shows.

Angie kept on living at the house
cooking breakfast, mopping floors,

playing Gin Rummy with Grandma,
until the day a man came knocking

on the front door. *Where's Angie?*

She got my baby up in there?
Grandma had no choice but to watch

the man steer Angie toward his El Camino.
Angie clamping the baby to her chest,

inhaling his scalp. Grandma sobbed.
Bert and Ernie chirped away on the TV.

III

Mom told about the time Grandma walked
out of Kroger's with someone else's child.
And the time she got busted shoplifting
baby clothes from Woolworth's.

By the time I was climbing out
of my bedroom window to smoke

and vanish along the railroad tracks,
Grandma had had it with the ghosts

of babies, sold her house and all its moaning,
crossed the Ohio to never cross back,

bought a small plot on Fish Gut Road, built
a coop with help from no man, raised

Leghorns and a few Rhode Island Reds.
She had showed me how to cut out snowflakes,

made a kick-ass bologna sandwich,
and could skin a squirrel in ten seconds flat.

She offered Mom $25,000 once
to raise me as her own.

I was nabbed for keeping up the family business—
shoving merchandise down my pants.

THAT GIRL IN THE NEWSPAPER, WE KNOW HER

In her arms a boy with a dirty face.
Under her dress another on the way.
They've been living out of a Buick
parked along the Ohio River. She stares

out of the pockmarked windshield
at a clapboard church. Yellow
foxtail grass and ragweed swallow
headstones. Sprigs sway and lull

the child. The graves resemble
unmade beds. She admires his eyelashes,
hums an old Appalachian hymn
my grandma taught her to sing.

The article says Child Services tried
to take him before, and that after dark
a man walking Memorial Bridge spotted
the Buick's headlights sinking below the water.

NEVER ASK WHAT'S UNDER THE BED

Your grandfather once shot a man,
my mother says over pea soup on the porch—
chucked his sorry ass down a well,
kept the man's false teeth as a souvenir.
Take that to your fancy school
for when you forget who you are.
The jobs have ditched town, and the freight
trains are gone—no longer rattling
windows, shaking nails from rotten studs.
The house shivers on its own.
We move out to the yard, squat down
on five-gallon buckets and scavenge fallen
pears among dandelions and bluegrass,
my favorite AC/DC T-shirt and my woodshop award
stuffed in a cardboard suitcase at my feet.
My generation, we didn't have learning
disabilities, we just drank homebrew,
and threw knives at each other.
Sweetness drips off her chin,
her mouth a honeycomb of bees.

AFTER OHIO

The first summer living with Dad,
I dug out the septic system with shovel
and pick ax. It was to deter any dreams

of a career in ditch digging. I learned
how to spur climb a tree, and wield
a chainsaw thirty feet in the air. I traded

a butterfly knife for a guitar, taught
myself the blues. I was called a hillbilly,
and for the first time not affectionately.

Mom's voice cracked and contorted
over the phone, asking who I loved more,
if I still loved her, if I ever loved her at all.

Dear Josh,

*Frank got probation for five years, and has to go to AA meetings—
if he doesn't they can put him back in jail. He started working at
MacDonald's. Last Monday night Janet tried to leave Jerrod with
him. She said she had no other place—of course Aunt Debbie wouldn't
let Jerrod stay the night so I kept him Monday and Tuesday. Frank
walked him to school and Janet picked him up. I don't know where
they're living. I wish Frank never got mixed up with her. Eugene and I
had a garage sale last Saturday. It went okay.*

Love, Mom.

Mom used to wake me for school
flipping on the big ceiling light.
Get your ass out of bed.

I'm not dealing with your shit.
My stepmother ran her fingers
through my hair, brushed

my forehead until my eyes opened.
It happened only once, but enough for me
to want to rid myself from Ohio dirt,

skin the jean jacket from my back,
shear my mullet and hose down
every inch of this punk stain.

THE WRONG CROWD

The fat kid swaggered over
to my brother and his crew
in the park. He liked their BMX's,
bummed a cigarette. Liked the skulls
with serpent tongues sewn
on their jean jackets. He bragged
about how he and his cousin
hung a cat from a backyard tree.
Laughed as he pantomimed
the thrashing. Rocks and fists—
my brother, his friends joining in,
beat that boy until his screams
overflowed with spent teeth.

MOTHER, THESE AREN'T YOUR FLOWERS

I thrust open a stubborn window,
causing a book to plop on its side,
slide off the shelf and, washed over

by a wave of other books, crash
into a rose-filled vase that smacks
on the hardwood floor.

What follows is silence, the split
second after a mother slaps
her child. I'll let the water search

the valleys of the room, finger
the petal-thorns and prism-shards.
This isn't your carpet ruined

by spilt paint. You will not lean
in the doorway smelling of strawberries
and righteousness. No wailing

or pleading here, only the quiet
twinge of panic ingrained
by the memory of your nearness.

II

BAND PRACTICE

We huddled around a space heater in Casey's basement
and stumbled our way through a Charles Mingus tune.

December. Our hands shivered or they couldn't move.
We wore winter coats playing "How High the Moon."

Casey hunched over the piano his father hauled home
in a pickup. It was missing a B-flat and was out of tune.

Scott spilled silk from an alto sax with a dented bell
as I walked my bass on a waltz by Sonny Fortune.

We boogied through "Blue Christmas," for a show
that required us to play at least one Christmas tune.

Everything was riding on the *Holiday Extravaganza*
because we didn't have another gig booked until June.

We'd ditch school scrunched down in Scott's Camaro.
We needed extra practice. We were graduating soon.

Mill-town kids bored with heavy metal sludge
we wanted to taste the world with a new spoon.

DECEMBER

I'm next to the bathtub Jesus
in my pajama bottoms and unlaced
construction boots with panting
tongues. I jingle my keys, hold
a soggy paper plate of steaming tuna
to tempt the black cat out of the woods.
She skulks through the understory
straight to my flannel legs. I like to think
that somewhere beyond the trees
an old woman in a robe and fuzzy slippers
is striking a metal pot with a wooden spoon
hoping I'll stumble through the pines
so she can warm my cold hunger
and mother this feral heart.

AFTER OHIO

Josh,

Your grandmother liked the Christmas card you sent her. She said she is going to hang it on the wall. Here's a newspaper clipping she sent me about the big chemical fire they had in Maysville. Frank lost his job again. He just said people keep fucking with him. I don't know what that means. Well, take care.

Love ya, Mom.

I want nothing to do with Ohio
and its river of fire, its boneyards
of automotive plants, but I miss

tornado-green skies over cornfields
and drive-thru liquor stores. I live
where there's a bridge of flowers

and a mass grave deep in the woods
behind the asylum. Where four towns
were flooded to quench Boston's thirst.

I once found a dead cat on the side
of the road in a brown grocery bag.
I've never been abandoned by art.

NOTHING YOU CAN DO

For Chanel

I'm boring. I know this.
I wake early in the morning,
walk around in boxers and socks,
listening to a classic Blue Note recording.
You don't care for Coltrane, you
think socks and boxers unattractive,

but you're not here, so I spend hours
at the window, coffee, cigarettes,
watching the neighbor kick his dog
for digging up roses. I think about poems,
how many trees I could put in them;
birch, pine, hemlock, maple.
On the other side of the grove,

traffic rolls down the highway.
The interstate is a belt holding up
the greasy work pants of the world.
My fifth cup of coffee: I'm buzzing—
worried by the sugar rotting my teeth
and the way you'll say you love me
when you walk into the kitchen

after a day at the office:
I love you, Sweet Butt,
my box-of-imperfection,
my little ball-of-shit.
Grinning in the bathroom mirror,
I peel my lower lip down to my chin.
My teeth, sickly refugees huddled

on a tiny raft breaking apart in open ocean.
I teeter on the idea of calling a dentist,
but like a childish god I'm patiently waiting

for all my toys to sink to the bottom of the tub.
What did you do today? you'll ask,
flopping down a stack of paperwork.
Wearing a maroon bathrobe, I'll look

up from a Frank O'Hara poem, and say, *Nothing*.
You'll shake your head, run your hand
through my slicked back hair, and click-clack
into the next room with a *You're so boring*.

I'm transfixed by the miniature whirlpool
I create with a spoon. The earth whips
around the sun. I'm clinging to its pant-legs.

AIR GUITAR

Out of all my instruments, the most prized,
the one I allow no one to touch.

The color of sunlight and atmosphere,
and when tilted the right way,

as if you were going to play it like a violin,
the faint hint of turquoise. I perform best

with the blinds drawn and the lights off: the electric
lime of the Pioneer Reverberation Stereo Receiver

is enough to keep bare toes from jabbing into table legs,
knuckles cracking against doorjambs while windmilling.

After work, after I've uncorked the bottle,
the wine granting my first wish, I slide under the strap

and unravel my fingers on Wes Montgomery licks.
It's well past midnight when I staccato through the house,

chugging on "Hell's Bells" as I rock on my heels,
balancing on flame-tips. And it's long after

the bars on Pleasant Street have closed, the sidewalks
overflowing with feedback and faces bent out of tune

that I play along with the song they're humming,
the one about home, and how it's a quartertone,

somewhere between C and C#,
and how we remarkably find the right key.

FUNCTIONAL

My father won't read poetry. He taught
my brother the ways of paintbrush
and canvas, played guitar before I was born

but after Nam, lost interest, saw no sense
in art. I'd like to think, surviving war,
I'd see no better reason to create, proclaim
and praise *I am here*, but what do I know,

given my armed conflict with the self?
My father once cradled a dying soldier
missing everything below his waist,

and watched a starving boy convulse
after a sergeant handed the child a candy bar—
his body no longer understood food.

My father pulls shoulder muscles
as he masons walls, lays foundations.
He cracks knuckles against engine blocks,

torqueing wrenches. Because the dead
remind him that splinters in his palms
are gifts, he builds cabinets, chairs, houses.
His life is work, no room for self-indulgence

or anything frivolous. But don't we also live
in rooms not constructed out of lumber and stone?
Art is an alarm clock. Art is a ladle of beauty

lifted to the lips. My father. On the table
he planed, sanded, stained—where we've sat
together after a long time of not sitting together,
where we've eaten slow—I want him to dance

and afterwards, I want him to see the scuffmarks
on the pine as affirmations of purpose—of loving
the lost with raucous praise, of letting the gone go.

POME

I want to kiss your pomaceous everything,
lay you on the teacher's desk, and love you
sticky on my chin. Why when you worm
your way into my head do I taste nothing
but cider? When I try to formulate
the mathematical equation for God and hope,
you break me down into my lowest
common denominator: bobbing at your flesh,
biting through your rind. You leave me
bruised, but drive me delicious.

BLUES 13

I

Pine boughs sopping from rain,
sky gray as a face turned
toward the wall, freight train
rambling past the one-pump
gas station with the phone booth
that no longer has a phone.

II

You haven't had the blues
until your mother drunk-dials
your number at two o'clock
in the afternoon and leaves
a message for your brother
who's been dead since 2007.

III

She refuses to use her walker.
She fell out of bed again, broke
her collarbone. My stepfather
gets up from his chair
only to piss on the carpet.
Every day he asks after his son
and the farmhouse he shared
with his first wife. Mom tells
him that his son is dead.
She no longer reminds him sweetly.

IV

Our love's an old vinyl record
I pull from its yellowed sleeve
when no one's around.

V

Twenty years after Vietnam my father
walked the living-room walls
hand-over-hand in his sleep, searching
for hot spots, for the fire raging
on the other side, calling out the names
of his squad through the quilted breath
of our otherwise dark and silent house.

VI

We played the blues
badly down in Casey's
mother's basement, wrote
songs about working
at the Dairy Queen
and what a drag it was
trying to get laid,
using the "Hoochie
Coochie" riff we lifted
off the Muddy Waters
record we swiped
from the library. The blues,
just another pretty girl
who wouldn't speak to us.

VII

When the guitarist
made the note whine,
it was one of many stings.

VIII

When Angie toweled off her son
in the motor-lodge bathroom.
His Spiderman PJs folded
on top of their one suitcase.
The blinds drawn, door
chained. The panic she felt
every time a car slinked
through the parking lot.

IX

At the group home my client rams
his head through the wall. I offer
him a pill so the neighborhood kids
won't hide behind their mothers' knees
when he walks past their front lawns.
I keep a keen eye on the distance
between my hand and his teeth.

X

Was your light green,
or just a shade of blue?

XI

I'm tired of these smiling faces,
these damn gardenias. They're burning
tires at the dump, because their fathers
burned tires at the dump, black smoke
like a bad feeling—rising. The church
steeple always there sprouting through
the trees where a mob once hung a man
for grinning too long at the wrong woman.

XII

A blackbird in crosshairs, singing.

XIII

Midnight, and it's snowing
and it's 1992. My brother's
on the phone, the lights off.
His breath blooms and wilts
on a window. Janet's voice
fades in and out over the line.
She's going to leave the man
she left him for. This time,
once the roads are plowed,
she's coming home for good.

WE WALK THE GROUNDS

Abandoned State Hospital

Decades since he's screamed himself
awake within these walls. He points

to where the slaughterhouse stood,
swings an imaginary sledgehammer.
That building's where orderlies used to herd

patients into a room with a drain in the floor
to hose them down. We peek in the windows
of what was once the chapel. Dead flies

on the sill, black legs like bare branches
raking snow from the sky. The pews
and alter gone. Hundreds of wheelchairs,

some with IV poles, aligned back to back,
wall to wall. A walk through the woods
takes us to the unmarked graves

of over four hundred in a hayfield.
There used to be a memorial bench
with a bronze plaque flanked by yews

but vandals have stolen the plaque
and hacked the bench into splinters.

FATHER, SITTING AT THE KITCHEN TABLE IN THE DARK

You've burned your knuckles
pulling trays of blueberry
muffins out of the oven.
You've sucked on pain.

How many gingerbread
houses have crumbled under
their own sugary weight
before one poised, melted

butter in its windows?
I'm the snow that frosts
your roof and ledges.
Step out and show the stars

your steamy tongue. Listen
for the moon howling back
to the wolves. Rejoice!
Rejoice in your scars.

AFTER OHIO

Dear Josh,

I hope you liked your birthday gift. I wasn't sure which Merle Haggard CDs you had. I haven't heard from Frank in about three weeks. Debbie kicked him out of her place. I knew it was only a matter of time. She said he went to stay with Mark's cousin, Carlos. I don't think he's been working, so I don't know what he's been doing for money, and I don't think I want to know. I got word from down home that Mom isn't doing too well. I need to give her a call.

Love ya, Mom.

I get a call from back home
only when someone's dead
or in jail, or when my mother

passes out in the driveway
and lies six hours in the snow.
One painting is what's left

of my brother. What's the narrative
in a still life or a landscape?
Long after my parents are gone

that trombone solo in Sinatra's
"I Got You under My Skin,"
will call to me, blaring.

INTERNAL BLEEDING

Sliding my bare feet across cold linoleum,
yawning as I attempt to separate two coffee
filters like peeling skin away from skin,

I notice out the window, at the edge of the yard
where a patch of woods begins, a deer standing
like a lawn ornament among sheets of fog.

She lowers her muscular neck to the frosty grass,
steam rises from her muzzle, and I'm staring
into the shotgun barrel of her eyes, holding

my breath, waiting for her to pull the trigger.
For endless seconds a soft wind rocks
the finger-smudged window gently

in its frame. The muscles in my neck
and shoulders unravel from the bone.
The moon shines like wolf teeth.

The deer darts off into the thicket,
carrying her kill—my heart pounding
with every silent step of her hooves.

III

LOVE YOU LIKE BREAD

Clouds shroud the city like newspaper
over an old man's sleeping face. The wind

teethes on our ears, drizzle needles
our cheeks. A gnarly loaf of challah

steams from a brown paper bag nestled
in my coat. *The shuk is a zoo on Fridays,*

you say, *everybody shouting and pushing.*
You relive Jerusalem, roam Emek Refaim

in your head, the coffee from its cafés
fresh on your taste buds, you fall

in love again and again. I rip off an end.
The sesame seeds are Braille for the tongue,

naming each little explosion in the mouth:
sourdough, brown sugar, pinch of rosemary.

We should go to Israel, you say. My silence
gives the same answer it gave in the past.

Minor thirds of disappointment
wheeze from your chest and I'm sorry

I'm not who you sometimes wish.
The challah's crust—a soft crunch,

like walking on frosted grass, then
a featherbed for the teeth. *I'll visit you*

in New York, I say. Your arm tightens
around mine, lips curl into an okay.

We've survived the pastries, the lard
and artificial flavoring of relationships.

We work with simple ingredients.
Want more? I say. Your hand reaches in,

and I grip the bag so you can wrestle
off a bigger piece.

AFTER OHIO

Hi Josh,

Same old news with Frank, can't or won't get a full-time job, but of course if you sleep 'til 3pm, you can't find a job like that. He keeps asking for money, and I keep telling him no. He's supposed to do jobs with Uncle Lanus, but with Frank his money goes fast. He got a letter from Child Support. I don't know what it's about, but I can guess. Since he lost his job at the Sheraton, over two years ago he hasn't been paying his support. I hope things are going well with you.

Love, Mom.

I was never good at foreign tongues,
failed both Spanish and Italian. Jazz
is a language no one I knew

knew how to speak, which was why
I wanted to speak it—how it wrangles
chaos, gives it form. But my mother's words

had become gibberish. So distant
I've hurled myself from her world
and I learned how to say *I love you* in Hebrew.

DAVE BRUBECK

You can hear the youth of his heart
in the pouncing of his block chords.
He's a kitten when it comes to his ball
of twine. At ninety, not to say

his melodies are arthritic,
or his left hand falls asleep
in mid-conversation with the right.
The felt-tipped hammers drive each note

into a surefooted place. Harmonies shift,
easy as sunlight progressing across the carpet.
He's in time with complete being,
strength and weakness syncopated

within one opus, the life-energy of jazz.
I questioned my own offbeat rhythms.
Now I know what key I'm in.
Tonight, I'll sleep like a pillow.

STAY

I seldom leave my apartment,
except when necessary, to borrow
jazz CDs from the library

or to grab a bite at the diner
with plaster cow heads
protruding from its marquee.

I leave and end up swerving
my blue Corolla to avoid hitting
a black bear climbing

over a guardrail, or stomping
on my brakes two feet from Nerissa Nields
who's double-fisting Starbucks

and jaywalking. I leave to meander past
Sylvia Plath's black–shuttered house
and Dickinson's grave. I'm still waiting

for my song. I leave to hear Dean Young
read poems about avian
affairs and his heart transplant.

Leave when it's time to walk
the old rail bridge over the river—to glance
down and long to disappear in its flow

or to stroll the old neighborhood
with my love, searching for ghosts
of our younger selves. The worst

is when I must leave—but today
I don't have to have tires rotated,
or cavities filled. Which is why

I want her to shred her bus ticket to New York,
rub my head, and report on the day's hustle
and traffic at the birdfeeder.

AFTER OHIO

Dear Josh,

Janet has moved in with her dad and stepmom. I'm so glad. She's been living here and there, even tried moving in with Frank and Aunt Debbie, but Debbie wouldn't have it. At least Jerrod will have a warm bed and food. When I picked him up two weeks ago, he hadn't had anything to eat all day. He was starved! Frank wanted me to call him at the bar. He left a message saying that big shit was going down. Well every time he and Lanus get drunk big shit goes down so I didn't call him. Let me know when you're graduating. I know your life will work out just great. It's good to have good friends. It's good to have someone there to give you a helping hand.

Mom.

I fell in love with a girl with braces
and bangs hair-sprayed in the shape
of a striking cobra. We used to park

at the lake in her grandma's Renault.
She told her grandma that the stain
on the backseat was from ice cream.

Backwards white trash, low-life
peckerwood, but the first in my family
to graduate college. Why do you

think I can fingerpick "Blue Monk,"
on the banjo, swing "Ol' Joe Clark,"
on bass, and play Bach Preludes on both?

MY GRANDPA'S BANJO

"All music is folk music. I ain't never heard no horse sing a song."
                                       —Louis Armstrong

My thumb plucks a string.
My other fingers slide
from note to note, then pull

off and let the sound ring.
Picking fingers are wild
horses galloping and rolling

across a drum-skinned moon.
As a teenager I winced
at its tin-twang nature

and toothless connotations.
Implication of a white
hooded robe hanging

somewhere in your closet;
me, playing razor-sharp
jazz to cut blood ties—*I'm*

not one of them.
But time changes keys.
Bela Fleck's a fusion force

smelting bluegrass with jazz
and the roar of blenders.
Carolina Chocolate Drops

fiddle "Genuine Negro Jigs"
and turn hip-hop into jug
tunes. And when Willie Nelson

sings the blues with Wynton Marsalis
my heart wants to bust out
of its stable and thunder through

open prairies. Oh music,
to be unbranded, to buck free
and far from the paddocked mind.

HEAVEN IN THE DEVIL'S HOUSE

For Lea Banks

Let me be a bead of sweat dangling
from a bluesman's nose.
Let me splash, absorbed

by the sawdust on the bone-creak
floorboards. Let wee-hour bodies
cling to one another with limp limbs

as they slow drag to a blood-thump
beat. Let the room be smothered
in smoky chords and moans

until sun seeps out of the swamp
to halo the cypresses. Let the spirits
of Bessie Smith and Skip James blaze

through windows clouded
by the soot of torch songs to touch
the tired, glistening faces.

IF YOU MUST ASK

I'd rather talk about love sprouting
over a shared cupcake between strangers
than explain how Chanel and I live
in separate houses in different states.

When I was a kid my father fretted
over mortgage payments, afraid
the bank would snatch our house
right off its foundation while we slept.

I vowed to never buy a house.
My father warned that as an adult
I wouldn't have the time
to play guitar, write poems.

I'd have a family to support, a yard
to maintain. I decided never to marry.
No kids. I haven't raked a leaf
since 1995. Chanel fears patriarchy

and hates children. Loves feeding stray cats.
What we have is sixteen years of separate
bank accounts and a shared bliss
in ice cream and true-crime TV. A mutual

understanding that if forced to choose
between art and each other, art wins—
so it's our own best interest to keep
the other's art happy. We drive

to the coffee shop and claim opposite ends
of the room. She'll finish her essay
for Cosmo, about how her 30s
are like other people's 20s, or redraft

the chapter in her novel about Israeli
settlements. For me, attempting the poem
I've tried to write for my stepmother
that I've never been able to compose.

Five hours later I catch her eye
and point to my gaping mouth, signaling
it's time for tacos and strawberry mojitos.
What's not owned can't be taken.

TWO TEENAGE BOYS AT A PICNIC TABLE

One with blue eyes and spiked bleached hair
slices an orange-frosted cupcake with a plastic knife,
and plops half on the napkin in front of the other—

short-sleeved flannel shirt and red shoes.
The blond sits tall and straight while the other
hunches with his chin in the crux of his arms.

As his eyebrows bounce in a playful Groucho Marx
kind of way, the one with the knife licks icing
off the blade. The other glances over his shoulder,

then tugs the napkin to drag the treat closer.
He picks it up gently, cranes his neck to bite
the bottom, saving the sweetest for last.

The one blessed with baby blues slides his arm
across the table, reaches for the other's free hand.
The flannel-clad boy pulls back, but then lays

his arm close enough for their arm hairs to share
a kiss of electricity, close enough for them
to feel the heat radiating from their skin.

STRENGTH TRAINING

    I'm a slouch.
        I've an anchor-heavy
     head
          that lives
              to sink.
    Blame my ironless blood.
        Slice a vein?
  I'll never rust.

    My mind—
        a basin
  full of dirty dishes.
            I'm out of soap.
          Meaning
I can only think in shades
    of brown and orange.

Imagination's my instrument.
        Sometimes I talk
with the eloquence of daytime television.
    Sometimes everything I say
  has the aftertaste of prune juice.

              But
I broadcast my shadow puppets
    on a bedsheet stretched
            between two trees
even when the flashlight's run
    out of juice.

IV

SNOW ANGELS

Each night they stare into the sky
and wonder why even with wings
they can never get off the ground.
Good reason for their creator
to take three steps, cock his head
and disown his gift to the world.
Abandonment: a likely origin of anyone's
lack of faith. And faith: precisely what's needed
to soar in the purple abyss of winter.

We step out into our lives like sun slicing
between buildings and perform this one angelic
act that melts from our consciousness.
We return to our houses to accomplish
something important, leaving behind
the ones who don't know any better,
who see the wings as open arms,
snow as flesh, and are willing to lie back down.

MOTHER, THE LATE-DECEMBER SUN IS AN OLD MAN

with a heavy head. 2:30 in the afternoon,
and he's laying himself down behind
the pines. Snow outlining the branches

makes me think of music (everything
makes me think of music), the silence
between the notes giving melody its shape.

There's a woman who plays steel drums
in front of the pizza joint for jingle money.
She wears a fur coat and one of those huge hats

southern women put on for Sundays. Her tunes
resemble church bells, wind chimes,
and metallic birds. Every time I hear a train

whistle and the click-clack of steel wheels
on a track, I think of you. It always sounds
far off, even now, as I stand on the platform

of the abandoned depot with Amtrak-silver
blurring past, you're still in the distance, a light
on the horizon that never arrives, never fades.

JANUARY

Trees cluster outside your window
like villagers with pitchforks.
The house reeks of old books
crammed with dirty thoughts.

Everything tastes of cough syrup.
Only the ghosts of the park statues
frolic on the swings while the homeless
mill about dressed as pigeons.

Yet there's always the young woman
sloshing towards the hacking bus.
Always the sunflower handbag
planted in the furrow of her chest.

AFTER OHIO

Josh,

Well two weeks ago Frank was put back in jail for violating his parole. Just before Halloween he got a job washing dishes at the Yacht Club, but of course that's now gone too. He spent Christmas in jail, and will be there until sometime after New Year's. I hope you had a good Christmas.

Love, Mom.

When scoring a revolver from a guy
who lives out of his car, you don't plan
much of anything else for that day.

And when he doesn't show up
you wander into the bookstore
near where he promised to park

and, since you're looking for any reason
for anything, you thumb through a book
of poems because the cover resembles

an old jazz album, and you buy the book,
never the gun, and if someone asks if poetry
has saved your life, you know what to say.

TORTURE, BROTHER

With every charley horse you
walloped into my thigh, a cackle.
Worse was when you'd straddle
my chest and hock a loogie

into my face. You grilled a mean
steak & egg sandwich—I'll give you
that. I tell everyone how you pulled
a switchblade on the kid who pushed me

off the slide. I wanted to be you,
right down to the cigarette pinched
between your fingers: a little rebellion
rising at the gates of your mouth.

But now you shit yourself and keep
lost teeth in a leather jewelry box.
Mom says you look as if you just
walked out of a concentration camp,

but watching you sleep I think, *baby
bird*, and then of the times I huffed
under your weight, *someday I'll be bigger
than you*... Now, I contemplate the pillows

on the couch beside your hospital bed.
How easy. Not even a struggle. But then
I'm drawn to the silence in the room.
You've stopped wheezing. Hours churn—

clocks are liars. You crack a yellow eye,
lift one brow, the way you do, and spit.
*What the fuck you staring at?
Get me my smokes.* And I do.

WATERCOLOR ON CANVAS

"It's a joy to be hidden, but a disaster not to be found."
— D. W. Winnicott

My brother painted it back in high school:
a bottle washed up on a beach. It won
a Governor's Prize, hung in the statehouse,
all that talk of a scholarship. Everyone

assumes ocean, a crab's-eye-view—but
the shore is those flat stones we'd skip
across Lake Erie. Dad taught him
how to paint the sky, but it was the shadows

Frank loved. After he lost another job,
during each stint in jail, he'd give the painting
to an uncle or a sober friend for safekeeping,
so he couldn't hawk it for a fix. A week after

his funeral we found it in his closet. Inside
the bottle there's a letter. If you squint
you can make out the ghost-lines of script
done in pencil, then erased.

SOMETHING TO DO WITH VULNERABILITY

Frank H. Stewart, IV (1969–2007)

I like to look at the back of people's heads.
It's how I sense innocence. Maybe

it's that I can't see their eyes and teeth.
Watching my cat lap his water, I recall the gazelle

on TV lowering its head to the river, snatched
and shredded by a crocodile. I lock my doors.

At night the cat kneads my chest until he coils
himself, wedges his nose under my chin.

I hold my breath, listen to him purr and when
I begin to breathe again I watch this lifeboat

afloat on its human ocean. The experts
say he's in it for the body heat, nothing to do

with love. I wonder if we're any different.
I have to decide if imitation's enough.

He's still purring and I watch his body
rise and fall. We're both adrift.

I tell him I love him. I say it as if
there's somebody else in the room.

HARSH WINTER

The landscape's a few black strands of hair
on a white pillow. From the window over
the kitchen sink, we watch a buck at the edge
of the yard strip bark off the trees. Last week
they wheeled Mrs. Green out on a sheet-draped
gurney. The paramedics said they could see
their breath inside her house. Here we are,
side by side, with soapy hands finding each
other in dishwater. The woodshed's shadow
stretches across snow pinked by the sun.
Come spring our souls will be like the long
road out of town: muddy, full of ruts,
but still the only passage to the orchards.

REACH

A priest storms out of an old woman's house,
handkerchief pressed to his face, fleeing
before giving the last rites, unable to stomach
gangrene that turned her feet into charred wood.
Diabetes set fire to nerve endings, cursed her
with tremors that fluttered her hands like flames.

As a girl, she broke through pond ice, sprawling
her arms, catching edges of the hole. Ice gave way
under her weight. Waterlogged skates nagged her ankles.
The wind rumbled—measuring the vastness. No swoosh
of traffic, just splashes, and the echo of splashes.
She stopped, clung to what there was to cling.

Her heart beat slow and slower. She heard her body say
sleep. Then a voice from behind—the boy from the trailer
in the cove crawled onto the pond, extending
a beanpole from the clothesline.

Her brother once tripped this boy flat on hockey ice.
She'd laughed. He smelled of dirty laundry, went
to a special school. His mother strutted into
The Angry Moose midmornings, slumped over the bar
by late afternoon. Townies talked about how
she'd kick him out of the trailer
when she entertained farmhands or loggers.
Drive by at night, and you'd see him
hunched over a campfire, even in winter.

The old woman remembers waving from her canoe
as she skimmed past his place the following spring.
Dusk. He was snapping twigs for kindling,
the sun turning the ripples into white gold.

She wanted to touch the mouth that tried
to swallow her whole.
                      She's lifting her paddle,
cleaving the water with her fingers
when her husband walks into her room,
presses her hand to his face, begins to sing

her favorite hymn. Water's edge, the boy
gives her a nod, then works deeper into the woods.
She looks out toward the cattails and reeds.
Water laps against the canoe.
She listens to the loons. Pushes on.

V

LOVE MUSIC

It starts with a fever in your pants,
ends with a one-way conversation

with a cigarette. I'm a bottle of blues
floating in your boogie-woogie.

This is what it's come to: the slow groove
of my heart, listening to Frank Sinatra

on a winter morning with the blinds drawn,
Count Basie slumped over the piano

tapping the black keys—those naked
little branches, sinking them in snow.

WE CALL IT US

Unwrap the sockeye from the butcher's paper,
brush the orange-pink flesh with olive oil,

sprinkle sea salt, black pepper, and minced garlic.
Lay the fish skin-side down on the cedar plank

that we steeped overnight in white wine and lemon juice.
Let it all smoke slowly on the grill while we unfold

our bodies like beach towels, spread them out
on patio chairs. Father, call this happiness, but

when we had nothing, we had wild flowers
in a mason jar on the warped kitchen table.

I WANTED TO BE A BLUE JAY OR WEAR A FLOWERED APRON

Steam rises from my coffee like fog off a lake.
This must be how the pond near our home appeared
as my father stood, with the suicide note I had written
in his coat pocket, scanning the calm water for a scar.
But I was behind the shed in the backyard,
taking swigs of vodka, shoving Vicodin into my mouth.
Blue jays flew in and out of the pines.
I delighted at their squawking—thought of tenement women
airing laundry on fire escapes.
I wanted to climb the branches for the same reason

I wanted to walk into a house of strangers when I passed
the glow of their kitchen windows—to sink into their lives,
their chicken soup. Didn't William Matthews compare
heaven with the eternal light of talk after dinner?
After awhile I heard footsteps wading through the leaves.

I waited for him to come around the shed, for his shadow
to cool the side of my face where the sun had been. But
why think of this now at Mocha Maya's on Halloween?
Hordes of plastic jack-o-lanterns stuffed with sugary loot
zip between tables while parents order extra shots
of espresso and compliment the costumes,
especially the mouse and her sister, the cheese.

One year I dressed up as a haunted house
my father constructed out of cardboard, rigged
with a tape recorder playing loops of creaking
doors and ghastly moans. There was even a chimney
with real smoke. These days when I bring him
pork braciole, when our plates are empty except
for a smearing of sauce, he takes us back
to that morning behind the shed, looking at me

as if I'm a jig-saw puzzle and he's lost the picture.
I didn't take into account that he'd blame himself,
that, with or without death, guilt would haunt him.
I wish I could tell him that love was enough
and the reasons why it wasn't. I want him to know
that once the dishes are cleared from the table
nothing rests between us except for our folded hands.

DEVOLUTION

My coffee's cold as a frog's belly,
and I'm daydreaming about shoving
small, slimy things into my mouth,

which sickens me with the urge
to reconnect with my ancestors, the ones

with webbed hands and feet, that breathed
through gills and sported undeveloped nostrils.
In the darkness of my windowless bathroom,

I light a candle and the flame emits a pulsing
glow against seashell tiles, and I think

of the caves where forebears harnessed fire
and chiseled stone into tools, then stepped out
and lifted their hands towards a galaxy

of other cave fires burning in a tundra
of sky, and, through guttural grunts,

gave birth to hope. More than walking
upright or burying our dead, our ability to see
life as something unfinished, in need of sanding,

separates us from the feathered and fanged.
It's what drives us to strive. I'd always thought

when nothing but ghosts finally stood between us,
my mother would spot my abandonment
across the room the way you can see the beating

hearts of those blind fish with translucent bodies
that live in cavern lakes below the earth.

'ROUND MIDNIGHT

For Bob Lipton

When some millennial breaks a poem
into lines of interpretive dance at the open mic,

Bob shatters spot-light silence, shouting,
Those sinuous hand moves look pretty lame.

And when the young poet challenges him
to a fistfight for dismantling his pride

in front of the girl in the maxi skirt, he pulls
a cigarette from his shirt pocket and says,

*Do you think your poetry will improve
if you beat on a member of AARP?*

A year to the day, police find Bob's body
alone in his bed. When someone leaves

your life, you're left with a story
you'll fetch from your mind's library

when sleep eludes you and you sit
in the quiet of the kitchen, surrounded

by the dark and empty rooms of self.
In the passage I keep flipping back to,

Bob and I are out front of the Hinge club.
He's finishing a smoke and I'm confessing

that my love for Dexter Gordon is greater
than my love for Coltrane, and Bob

is about to send poems off to Brilliant Corners
about how Monk would slouch

at his table between sets at the Five Spot,
and the kiss he shared with Annie Ross

at the Village Vanguard. We walk
to the corner mailbox and before he lets

the envelope slide down the chute he looks
at it for a long time and then presses

it to his lips, maybe wishing luck
to a part of himself he's sending out

to a world he isn't sure it's ready for, or
like saying goodbye to the girl he'd always loved

but never had the nerve to tell, or maybe
he does it by rote—like his sister used to do

during the war when she'd mail her heart
and promises to GIs sent over to Korea.

NOVEMBER MORNING,
HE COMES BACK UNEXPECTEDLY

I shuffle down the driveway to greet
the newspaper sheathed in plastic.
My breath twirls with the steamy hazelnut
of my cup, and my knuckles burn
against fired clay. The buzz of streetlamps,
the swish of cars two blocks over.
Across the street the neighbor's boy flicks
the porch light on and off, waves hello
in flashes, a game I'd play with my brother,
using wristwatch beams at bedtime, a memory
I'd forgotten, but have been given back.
A blessing wadded up and stuffed in a wallet
behind a picture of someone lost, but loved.

AFTER OHIO

To Bro—

Do me a big favor and give Dad a big hug for me. I need to talk to you about Jerrod. Janet got in trouble, she took like $1,500 from her work. She's looking at jail time. So I think I'll get Jerrod. If I pass away before he turns 18 would you think about taking him? Just think. I don't want him in a home. Getting out of Sandusky, getting out of Ohio like you, would be the best thing for him. This town is rotten. Give me a call sometime. I know it's been a long time. Sorry.

Your bro, Franklin H. Stewart IV

I know how to run a washing machine
and paddle a canoe. I know how to kick
my feet to keep my head bobbing.

Here's a secret: the one who broke
through the ice was me, and the rescuing
was self-served, so I was the boy too.

I can tell by its tune what kind of bird
is in your tree. I can bake cornbread,
and bring you some. What do I know about
raising a kid, lost, and almost grown?

I think I'm going to buy a ukulele,
                       and teach myself
"The Ani Ohev At Atzmi Blues,"
and "Ain't Nobody's Business If I Do."

MY BROTHER'S SON

For Jerrod

You were fourteen when they wheeled
your dad's hospital bed into the living room,

you bathed his swollen feet, watched
as he turned away from the sun, a drooping

sunflower. Your grandma told me you slept
for hours on the couch beside him, unaware

of the unblinking eyes until you stood up
to rearrange the blanket that had fallen to the floor.

At the funeral, craggy-faced men you'd never met
patted the shoulders of your borrowed jacket.

I've dreamt of your dad only once since his death.
I'm looking out a picture window. He approaches,

wading through clumps of matted leaves and twigs.
He's as I remember him: jean jacket and biker boots,

flesh, hair and teeth returned. He mounts the porch,
his breath grows and fades on the glass, *Let me in*.

I shake my head. He stares.
Boy, I said, let me in. My face says *No*.

He pounds the window. It wobbles in its frame,
but I don't budge. *It's because you're dead,*

Frank. It's because you're dead. His arms hang.
For a long while, we stand there, two trees

on opposite sides of a stream that have spent
winter after winter silent and naked.

Without looking up from the porch planks,
or saying another word, he plods across the yard.

The last time I saw him before he got sick—a glass
partition between us at the county jail. That was the first time

you met your father. You sat in my lap, the phone's
earpiece covering half your head, holding the receiver

with both hands. After he hung up and shuffled off,
your eyes broke wide: *That him? Is that my dad?*

For years I didn't speak to him, miles between us.
Everyone said I'd regret not making amends,

but even now I'm relieved to know the cops
won't burst through the door with warrants.

Your grandma won't have to make calls
every time she hears about an unidentified body

on the news, and I'm relieved to know
that when he was too weak to raise his head,

you were there to hold a straw up to his lips
that the last thing he witnessed was kindness.

I TRIED TO HATE YOU
BUT LOVE YOU JUST THE SAME

My days are spent keeping a blind cat
from pissing on the rug and nights listening
for the fat in Ray Brown bass solos.

I used to drink coffee with cream, now
I drink it black. I cancelled my gym
membership. Progress. Regression.

I've been accused of being flippant,
my banjo out of tune, thoughts deep
as the frying pan my beef-patty's

sizzling in. Time to be serious.
I've an uncle with black lung
and arthritis so bad he can't button

his shirt. Dear Poets, we're not sages.
We're battered spouses of hope—
even when it blackens our eye

we rush back into its arms.
When you have nothing, you depend
on nothing the most. I want Lake Erie

to burn for old time's sake. Give me
flat fields and grain elevators. Scrape
under my fingernails and find rust

and brick-dust from abandoned auto
plants. Mother, I lost you
long before I'll ever lose you.

I'm not interested in last words,
but in final thoughts. Do you love
the most the one you think of last?

Are we defined by what shames us?
I'll work overtime to be a figment
of your imagination. I'll even moonlight

as one of your psychotic episodes.
We could've both been better angels
to one another, but Hell lives in the bones.

ONCE AGAIN LAKE ERIE

After Eugénio De Andrade

A ferry chugs across Sandusky Bay.
Its steel deck plates are the red

of a child's painting. Lake Erie,
its green water and fish carcasses

no longer in my life, but tonight
I'm twelve again, walking down

East Water Street, where shirtless
men in cutoff jeans flirt with other men

as the sun gleams and turns the white bricks
of office buildings into a salmon color

harmonious with the silent crawl of shadows
and the cry of seagulls. I'll clamber

over boulders of the revetment, where foundry
workers perch themselves to hook channel cat

and walleye after a long day of casting liquid
iron. Ferris-wheel lights on the horizon,

saltwater taffy on my memory's tongue,
and the strawberry-glossed lips

of a girl in a stonewashed mini skirt
and jelly shoes. So much kissing!

Fear of death and the exhilaration of living
swap saliva at the top of a rollercoaster.

GHOST NOTES

In my head the album never recorded:
Hendrix and Coltrane are two hawks
in a canyon, fighting midair over the same prey,

tearing at the flesh of a note that does not exist
while thunder from hammering minor chords

on a piano echoes off walls of rock and clay.
Elvin Jones is a river. He's drowning
in his own current of energy, flails his arms

above white-water cymbal crashes. I'm a man
that swims in wonder and augmented memories.

I've no use for the mapped-out terrain
of a symphony, or the prim etiquette
of a minuet. Give me the oldest folksong

and I'll embellish every phrase. Come hear
me play. Let down your red loose curls.

Shed your yellow summer dress. Open
your hymnbook, and I'll improvise
the dirtiest blues over holy harmonies.

Unlatch your ribcage. Take your instrument
from its beat-up case. Build yourself a stage

in the middle of a field, they'll come
not to hear you sing, but for you to wail
until dried blood flecks off the fretboard,

until you grit your teeth,
until you break every string.

ACKNOWLEDGMENTS

Grateful acknowledgment is made to the following journals where many of these poems were published, sometimes in different versions: *Cold Mountain Review, Connecticut River Review, Camroc Press Review, Country Dog Review, DMQ Review, Evansville Review, Flint Hills Review, Fried Chicken and Coffee, Georgetown Review, Gertrude, Great Lakes Review, Heat City Review, JMWW, Louisville Review, Massachusetts Review, Meat For Tea, Naugatuck River Review, Night Train, Pedestal Magazine, Pirene's Fountain, San Pedro River Review, Silkworm, Stickman Review, This Literary Magazine, William and Mary Review, Worcester Review, Word Riot.*

Some of these poems were first published in the chapbooks, *Vintage Gray* (Pudding House Publications, 2007), and *Sink Your Teeth into the Light* (Finishing Line Press, 2012)

"My Brother's Son," was published in the Anthology *Voices from the Porch*, edited by Maureen Sherbondy (Main Street Rag, 2014)

I would like to express gratitude to Steve Strimer, publisher of Levellers Press and its poetry imprint Hedgerow Books.

Thanks to all the Hedgerow readers for selecting my manuscript for publication, and Diana Gordon for her suggestions in editing this book.

A heartfelt thanks to Chanel Dubofsky, and to my parents for their love and encouragement.

Thanks also to Doug Anderson, Lea Banks, Paul Richmond, Lori Desrosiers, and to all my other beloved poets of the Pioneer Valley.

A very special thanks goes to Ellen Doré Watson, who's been my mentor for over fifteen years, and more than instrumental in the revising and editing of these poems. She has believed in my poems and my abilities as a poet even when I doubted both. Someone once said that poetry was the art of using words to express what words cannot express. To have the words to articulate my deepest appreciation for Ellen would be the poem I will forever be trying to write.

AUTHOR

JOSHUA MICHAEL STEWART was born in Sandusky, Ohio and moved to Massachusetts to live with his father and stepmother when he was thirteen years old. He received his BA from the University of Massachusetts, Amherst, and lives in Ware, Massachusetts. He's employed as Teacher/Counselor, working with individuals with special needs.